Printed in Great Britain
by Amazon

*There are significantly more than 99 Tips

You picked up this book so I am betting that like me you want to become better at spearfishing. You are not alone as thousands of spearos share the same desire. To consistently improve you need to spend lots of time in the water as well as spending time reflecting at the end of every dive day on what you could do differently next time. This guide will give you information to make this process easier.

Rather than being a comprehensive guide to every facet of spearfishing this guide incorporates short, highly practical tips into an easy to digest format for you to reflect on and adapt into your own spearfishing.

For a continual source of new information about everything from improving your breath hold to learning a new hunting technique join us at http://www.noobspearo.com/

Turbo and I would love to hear how some of these tips have improved your diving, email one of us turbo@noobspearo.com or shrek@noobspearo.com and tell us your story!

Spearfishing the world over is conducted in similar ways however every area of the world has developed specific techniques and styles to suit the local conditions. The Greek and Mediterranean divers are some of the deepest divers in the world. The Portuguese, Norwegians, Kiwis, and many others have adopted specific practices for diving in dirty water. Australians, Americans, and South Africans have developed some of the best equipment for taking down hard fighting pelagic fish. From all over the world spearos have dived, adapted and speared fish successfully and have their own stories, tips and insights to share.

Here are 99 Tips to whet your appetite and help you to dramatically improve your spearfishing.

Author

LEVI 'TURBO' BROWN

Author

ISAAC 'SHREK' DALY

Disclaimer and Copyright Page

The information contained in this guide is for informational purposes only.

We are not Freediving or Spearfishing Instructors. Any spearfishing and freediving advice that we give are our opinions based on our interviews and our personal experience. You should always seek the advice of a professional before acting on something that we publish or recommend.

The publication of such Third Party Quotes and information does not constitute my guarantee of any information, instruction, opinion, tips or services contained within the Third Party Material.

No part of this publication shall be reproduced, transmitted, or sold in whole or in part in any form, without the prior written consent of the authors. All trademarks and registered trademarks appearing in this guide are the property of their respective owners.

Users of this guide are advised to do their own due diligence when it comes to spearfishing and freediving and all information should be independently verified by qualified professionals. By reading this guide, you agree that Noob Spearo Pty Ltd is not responsible for your safety in any way relating to the information provided in this guide.

ISBN: 978-0-6481596-0-5

ABOUT THE AUTHORS AND PREFACE

Isaac "Shrek" Daly Co-hosts the Noob Spearo Podcast alongside Levi "Turbo" Brown in Brisbane, Australia. Originally from New Zealand with lots of time spent in and around the water with Scuba Diving, Life Saving and Swimming his keen interest has made him a passionate spearo.

Levi 'Turbo' Brown is the smaller half of the Noob Spearo Podcast (more like quarter). With his background in Environmental Science and passion for the marine environment, Turbo offers a unique and often humorous insight into Spearfishing.

ABOUT THE BOOK AND NOOB SPEARO

Spearfishing is a sport that has one of the steepest learning curves imaginable.

"Turbo and I both encountered lots of obstacles getting started spearfishing and so we created the Noob Spearo to help people overcome their own hurdles" - Shrek

"When I got started spearfishing I knew nothing, no one, had terribly ineffective equipment and had plenty of dramas with everything from equalizing to losing big fish. I enjoy learning and sharing with others what I have learnt." - Turbo

NOOB SPEARO'S VISION

1. We aim to help reduce spearfishing deaths (too many young Spearo's lose their lives in preventable situations)

2. We aim to help develop the next generation of environmentally aware Spearo's

3. We aim to help spearfishing grow as a lifestyle sport, by developing community and relationships with Spearo's from all over the world.

4. We aim to help our readers shoot more fish and have fun

NOOB SPEARO PODCAST

The Noob Spearo Podcast features world-class spearos who share their hard-won wisdom and experiences with us in interviews shared for free at www.noobspearo.com and also on iTunes, Stitcher and TuneIn radio. Many of the tips in this book are direct from spearfishing experts, authorities and characters from all over the world who have featured on the Noob Spearo Podcast. More than 40 renowned spearfishing men and women have joined us on the show.

NOOB SPEARO BLOG

The Vault is the home of articles on everything from how to get started shore diving to how to hunt, shoot and land Spanish Mackerel. Guest contributors, feedback from our listeners and community and our own experiences are fueling an ever growing catalogue of tips, tricks, hacks, DIY guides and articles for the aspiring Spearo.

CORE VALUES

We don't believe in big-noting and speaking to new or up and coming Spearo's like they are a new kind of bacteria found on Shrek's feet during a hot summer. Forums and social media are full of Spearo's abusing and disrespecting one another, we don't go in for that at Noob Spearo. We like to share a laugh, enjoy our spearfishing, tell real stories and share lessons learned, while inviting the next generation of divers into a healthy, safe and sustainable relationship with this epic sport.

GET INVOLVED

If you have a message to share with Spearo's or want to be part of a healthy community, sign up to the Noob Spearo newsletter and join our community. Contributors are always welcome and some of our best information now comes from spearo's like you with helpful information to share.

Table of Contents

CHAPTER 1
Finding the Good Places to go Spearfishing

01 // FINDING THE GOOD SPOTS.

Use Google Earth to get a bird's eye view of potential new dive sites. If you have heard about a potential new dive location from a mate, local dive shop or somewhere else check it out for yourself using Google Earth. The best locations that are accessible from the shore are sheltered waters such as, the sheltered side of a headland or rocky point, the sheltered side of an island or perhaps a harbour or estuary.

Google earth is a great preliminary tool for assessing an area's potential for being a good dive location. Using Google Earth you can locate structure like reefs, sea walls, headlands and even parking spots. What Google Earth fails to do is communicate conditions like current, visibility, entry and exit points and how easily the area is swell affected.

In Southern Queensland these spots are few and far between, however in the Southern half of Australia there are many more shore diving locations. It depends on what part of the world you live in and the prevailing weather conditions. Even in sheltered waters you can still learn to start shore dive spearfishing before heading out into the open ocean.

02 // FINDING THE GOOD SPOTS.

Find a good dedicated spearfishing retailer, local spearo or spearfishing group. Facebook groups are another great source of knowledge. These experienced spearos will have invaluable knowledge about your local area. They will be able to tell you about variables such as current, swell, entry and exit problems, seasonal jellyfish issues, boat traffic etc. As you gain experience in an area you will begin to make connections about what works in that particular area and what doesn't.

Water clarity is an issue here in Queensland. We have trouble finding clean water particularly in a Northerly wind, in other areas there are similar unique factors. If you can't find a local guide to be your buddy, then the next best option is to take a screenshot of the area you are planning to dive from Google maps and take it into your local retailer. Often they can point out things about the area or refer you to someone who can. Marking out key things such as recommended entry and exit points on the screenshot map will help you when you arrive on the day.

a tip...

"USE NAVIONICS, A HANDY MARINE APP THAT PROVIDES ACCURATE MARINE CHARTS ALL OVER THE WORLD TO FIND YOUR NEXT DIVE SITE."

03 // FINDING THE GOOD SPOTS.

Use Navionics, a handy marine app that provides accurate marine charts all over the world to find your next dive site. Using navionics you can store any GPS marks that someone is kind enough to give to you. Another useful way to use the app is to observe bottom structure by paying close attention to irregularities and depth changes in the contour lines. Conveniently many reefs and wrecks are marked on the charts. There is a free service and a paid service. I recommend the paid service as the maps show more detail.

Our interview with Trevor Ketchion an experienced South East Queensland spearfisherman provided us with good information about how to use your charts and sounder. One tip that stood out was that when you have 2 or more good marks in a line away from a point of structure (on land) often the ground between these marks can be worth checking out, even if there is no easily identifiable reasons for doing so.

04 // FINDING THE GOOD SPOTS.

Government websites, line fishing websites, blogs and forums can yield some good information for spearo's scouting for potential spearfishing sites. Often recreational fishermen will find this information in the same place where they can locate local regulations and size limits (government sites). Line or pole fisherman also discuss spots online and sometimes their spots are not well known by spearo's. Offering a 6 pack of beer to a local commercial fisherman can also yield you a nice mark or two to explore next time you head out.

05 // FINDING THE GOOD SPOTS.

Tide, moon phase and time of day play a major role in how fish behave. Dawn and dusk are generally the most active times of day for all fish. Moon phase impacts species differently, often moon phases at specific times of year can signal a seasonal spawn.

Some fish species are at their most active in strong current and so can be targeted during times of large tidal variation. For other species it's the opposite, when the current increases, they disappear. These are all good reasons why you should keep a dive log - so that you can replicate good results and avoid the same scenarios where you achieved poor results.

a tip...
"KEEP A DIVE LOG - SO THAT YOU CAN REPLICATE GOOD RESULTS AND AVOID THE SAME SCENARIOS WHERE YOU ACHIEVED POOR RESULTS."

CHAPTER 2
Tips To Increase Your Bottom Time

06 //
INCREASING BOTTOM TIME.

Relaxation. Before you even get to the spot, do some full breaths to stretch your lungs and get your body prepared for diving. On the surface, close your eyes and concentrate on releasing all muscle tension. Hold your gun lightly in your hand and breath slow, deep and even. Go with the current and use the boat rather than swimming against the current when possible as this will keep your heart rate down.

A good buddy on the surface that you can trust will also help you to relax more. I know if Turbo's got my back I'm screwed. If you are diving from a boat in current than get dropped off just that little bit further up current so that you have more time to prepare and get relaxed.

Simon Trippe...

"IT'S TAKEN ME YEARS TO LEARN TO RELAX AND I STILL THINK THERE IS MORE TO LEARN". PROPER RELAXATION IS A LIFELONG FOCUS FOR BOTH THE HUNTING AND FREEDIVING FACETS OF SPEARFISHING.

Pre-Equalize on the surface. Once you have taken your last 3-4 slow full breaths, pre-equalize on the surface. This will give you a chance to complete your full duck-dive before having to reach up and equalize. And remember, early and often equalization will help you to be more relaxed when you reach the bottom. Squeezing hard stresses your body in many different ways.

 ## 08 // INCREASING BOTTOM TIME.

Good duck diving technique. The difference between a good duck dive and a poor duck dive can be measured in metres and makes a huge difference to your bottom time. Think hot knife through butter - be smooth. One way to make this actionable is make it a focus for your next dive day. Don't worry about improving everything at once, just nail your duck dive - it will make a huge difference.

Instead of doing the full handstand to begin your dive, try lifting just one leg. This will provide you with more than enough power to leave the surface and be ready for kicking. A good duck-dive will provide more thrust for less energy. A good freediving instructor will be able to teach you the proper technique.

09 // INCREASING BOTTOM TIME.

Better Finning Technique. When finning don't bend your knees. The movement should come from your hips and the stroke should be narrow to avoid drag. This is the most economical and effective finning technique. Get your mate to video you in the pool and try and get this right. A good freediving instructor is the best bet to help you improve this.

The difference between a poor finning technique and a good one means big differences in the amount of energy consumed and therefore oxygen and time on the bottom.

10 // INCREASING BOTTOM TIME.

Improve your streamlining. Water is more viscous than air so hydrodynamics play a huge part in increasing your bottom time. Lock your elbows into your body and tuck your chin into your chest (very slightly) to minimize drag and increase glide efficiency This is only for those of us that don't possess the blessed 'hands free' equalizing ability. Water is over 700 times denser than air, so failing to work on streamlining results in inefficient technique and decreased bottom time.

11 // INCREASING BOTTOM TIME.

Better Equalizing. Tucking your chin into your chest slightly, improves equalizing because your eustachian tubes will not be squeezed. Don't look up as you descend until close to the bottom (especially when diving deeper). Maintain early and often equalization and avoid forced equalization that can damage the ear drums. Forcing equalisation can increase oxygen consumption and increase your heart rate.

"SPEARO'S NOT ONLY HAVE TO STUDY THEIR QUARRY AND TERRAIN, THEY ALSO HAVE TO DEVELOP A BREATH-HOLD AND ECONOMICAL FINNING TECHNIQUE. IT IS THE BREATH HOLD AND GOOD TECHNIQUE THAT WILL GIVE THEM DEPTH AND DOWNTIME".

-Wayne Judge

FREEDIVING COACH & TRAINER

12 // INCREASING BOTTOM TIME.

Target Depth. Lifting your head as you descend is hard to avoid, but it is a major factor that separates the experienced from the inexperienced. Lifting your head before you reach your target depth creates more water drag and consumes more energy and oxygen that will decrease bottom time. It will also spook more fish.

> "SOMETIMES NOW WHEN I BEHAVE MYSELF AND LOOK UP ONLY WHEN I REACH THE BOTTOM, I AM SURPRISED AT HOW CLOSE PARROTFISH AND SIMILAR FLIGHTY SPECIES HAVE COME TO ME BECAUSE I HAVE BEEN IGNORING THEM".
>
> *-Shrek*

> "SO FOR THE GUYS (LIKE TURBO) THAT ARE DOWN THERE FOR THIRTY SECONDS, YOU WANT TO MAKE THE MOST OF YOUR TIME ON THE BOTTOM, RIGHT? SO INSTEAD OF DIVING DOWN AND LOOKING AROUND ON YOUR WAY DOWN, JUST GO STRAIGHT TO THE BOTTOM, AND ENJOY YOUR 20-30 SECONDS ON THE BOTTOM DOING SOME HUNTING INSTEAD OF ON THE WAY DOWN OR ON YOUR WAY BACK UP. I GUESS NUMBER TWO WOULD BE GO STRAIGHT FOR YOUR TARGET DEPTH, DON'T DILLY-DALLY IN BETWEEN".
>
>
> *-Roman Castro*

13 // INCREASING BOTTOM TIME.

Tuck your gun in close to your body reduce drag and minimise your profile in the water. Picture a soldier with his rifle beside his body. Any equipment or body part that sticks out creates drag and therefore energy and oxygen is wasted.

Look at your own profile in the water and make continual efforts to streamline. Pay attention to both your equipment and your technique. Watch your dive partners to improve your technique and offer guidance.

CHAPTER 3

Tips For Better Spearfishing Hunting Technique

14 // BETTER HUNTING TECHNIQUE.

Use your eyes to scan your surrounds without turning your head. This not only reduces oxygen consumption but spooks less fish! Relax your body and make sure you are on the bottom. When you try a head mounted camera you will notice how much that you move your head.

15 // BETTER HUNTING TECHNIQUE.

"Aspetto" refers to the method in which the hunter will lie on the bottom in wait for their prey. Spearo's using aspetto technique use smaller muscle groups to manoeuvre around on the bottom. This helps to conserve energy and therefore oxygen.

For example; if your buoyancy is completely neutral at 10m then moving forward to approach fish whilst on the bottom can be done with one hand lightly pushing off and propelling you forwards. In this way your entire body is not moving with the effort or the motion of finning, therefore you save on energy and are less threatening to fish.

16 // BETTER HUNTING TECHNIQUE.

Pelagic Hunting. Nearly always let the fish approach you, there are some exceptions to this rule but for the majority this is the rule.

17 // BETTER HUNTING TECHNIQUE.

Photo courtesy of David Ochoa

Better Hunting Technique. Honing your hunting instincts resides within your ability to observe your target species behaviour and to adapt accordingly. Here is a great example of studying and learning a specific species.

Dwayne Herbert, seven times New Zealand Spearfishing Champion, spoke to us about learning and mastering a species in a recent Veterans Vault section. He honed in on one specific reef fish, the New Zealand Boarfish that he identified as a challenging species to hunt. Like many spearfisherman he identified two critical factors.

1. What terrain, depth, season and locations are you likely to encounter your species?

2. What techniques will yield consistent good results for hunting that species once you are in the right area?

In the case of the Boarfish, Dwayne identified that spearfisherman encountered them in significantly larger numbers during seasonal spawns. He also got to know several hundred metres of reef quite well that contained the weed verges and overhanging structure ideal for holding these fish. Dwayne says he spent lots of time traversing the edges of reefs and observing these fish in their habitat. Paying attention to what times of day the fish were most active helped him to zero in on where and when to lie on the bottom in wait and what to do to arouse their curiosity.

The Boarfish Dwayne observed in these areas use their elongated snouts to dig in the sand on the weed edges of these reefs. While observing their behaviour he paid attention to where they fed, where they hid from predators, and where they were likely to be at specific times of the day. This information allowed him to develop hunting techniques for the various situations that you can hunt these fish.

Approaching them from above was a technique that he mentioned could be used on occasion however he stressed the need to get directly above them for an undetected approach. A more effective technique he identified was hiding his body in the weed and attempting to coax the fish in using several methods like dusting to arouse the Boarfish curiosity.

Paying attention over long periods of time and cataloguing that information has allowed Dwayne to hunt these fish with increasing proficiency over the years. Developing observational skills is about awareness more than anything else and these skills work for spearfisherman all over the world. Here are the three main considerations to think about when studying a new species.

*   What does this fish eat?

*   Where and when does this fish rest?

*   What hunts this fish and how does it avoid predation?

18 // BETTER HUNTING TECHNIQUE.

Better Hunting Technique. The Dusting Technique as coined by Reef Chief on reddit.com/r/Spearfishing/.

This technique is popular the world over and can often yield good results. It requires good bottom time and patience. Throwing sand up and pretending to pay attention to the bottom can mimic feeding reef fish behaviour and often other fish will come in to inspect the action.

Some fish such as Green Jobfish (Uku) will come in but it can be another incredibly taxing 20-30 seconds after you have thrown the sand up that they choose to show up. They seem to read a hunter's body language very easily and will stay just out of range. Which brings up a good point, no fish is worth your life and this technique is for the more advanced Spearo. This technique does however combine well with the next tip "scratching".

Photo courtesy of Jessie Cripps

Photo courtesy of Gabriel Wickens

"MY FAVOURITE TECHNIQUE IS DUSTING. CERTAIN CURIOUS SPECIES WILL COME IN TO INVESTIGATE STIRRED UP SAND. WORKS GREAT FOR SKITTISH HOGFISH AND MUTTONS. YOU SWIM DOWN, STIR UP SAND, AND WAIT FOR THE FISH TO GET CURIOUS."

- Reef Chief

 19 & 20 // BETTER HUNTING TECHNIQUE.

Scratching can be used in combination with dusting however this technique involves holding a piece of rock, hard coral or sand in your hand and roughly scratching it between your thumb and forefingers. The sound can arouse curiosity in nearby fish and they will come in for an inspection. Sometimes scratching and breaking up the hard coral and throwing it up a bit can all be done together to bring in curious fish. Beware of overdoing it. Try making quite a bit of commotion and then sitting completely still in the midst of it. Perhaps make small sounds but hide the source of the noise after your first flurry. This works particularly well with emperor species.

"WHEN SNOOPING SNAPPER, MAKE SURE THE SUN IS BEHIND YOU AND YOU SWIM SLOWLY INTO THE CURRENT LOOKING, SNEAKING OVER EVERY ROCK. GENERALLY SNAPPER WILL FLICK THEIR PECTORAL FINS OUT JUST BEFORE THEY BOLT AWAY. IF THEY DO THIS IT'S TIME TO SHOOT OR THEY ARE GONE!"

– Care of the Wettie team in New Zealand.

 ### 21 // BETTER HUNTING TECHNIQUE.

Remain active while on the surface.

"...USE YOUR EYES, IT SOUNDS FUNNY BUT YOU'D BE SURPRISED AT HOW MUCH GROUND YOU CAN COVER JUST WITH YOUR EYES. JUST WITH YOUR EYES AND YOUR HEAD. (IT'S) SOMETHING I'VE GOT TO CONSTANTLY REMIND MYSELF OF, BECAUSE IT'S VERY EASY TO GET LAZY WHEN YOU'RE IN THE WATER. YOUR HEAD JUST KIND OF FOCUSES ON THE BOTTOM, AND YOU CAN JUST BE SWIMMING. JUST KEEP YOUR EYES MOVING, KEEP SCOURING, SCOURING, SCOURING, GET THAT HEAD MOVING, YOU DON'T HAVE TO MOVE YOUR WHOLE BODY AROUND"

- Tanc Sade

22 // BETTER HUNTING TECHNIQUE.

Use noise to arouse curiosity. Chris Coates shared with our listeners a masterclass on using noise effectively for attracting fish. He says learning what noise to apply in each situation is something that comes with experience.

"...BECAUSE I KNOW THAT WHEN A SNAPPER TURNS AND HAS DECIDED TO GET AWAY FROM ME I CAN MAKE A SMALL NOISE AND HE WILL TURN. HOWEVER IF I CONTINUE TO MAKE THE NOISE HE WILL OFTEN CONTINUE ON HIS WAY, SO IT'S IMPORTANT TO MAKE THE NOISE BUT THEN BE SILENT WHEN HE LOOKS TO INVESTIGATE. IF HE TURNS, LOOKS, ,AND THEN CONTINUES I WILL START MAKING THE NOISE AGAIN AND BY THEN 7 TIMES OUT OF TEN HE WILL COME BACK FOR A DIRECT PASS TO SEE WHAT I AM DOING."

— Chris Coates

23 // BETTER HUNTING TECHNIQUE.

Newspaper Burley tip care of Manny Bova and Rob Gates. Using newspaper or tissue paper the same way we use ground fish frames in a steady, but slow stream can work just as well as real burley. The paper draws the light and attracts curious pelagic fish species to it like moths to a flame according to both of these Noob Spearo Podcast guests.

24 // BETTER HUNTING TECHNIQUE.

Exploiting the Blind Spot. If you are trailing a Mackerel there is a common Jedi mind trick that you can play on them provided the force is strong within you.

When you are trailing the fish, angle across behind the fish (from left to right) into its blind spot, and the fish will change course slightly so that it can get a good view of you. Do it again in the opposite direction and the fish should turn harder towards the opposite side presenting you with a broadside shot opportunity. Most species have a specific area of restricted vision that can be exploited. Observe and exploit!

Photo courtesy of Rob Allen

25 // BETTER HUNTING TECHNIQUE.

Flashers need to be worked up and down in mid-water within reach of the light. If the day is overcast and/or the water is a bit dirty then keep the flasher higher up in the water column. Have a little bit of distance between the divers and the flasher. Not so much that you can't keep active lookout for one another on dives but enough so that approaching fish don't get intimidated. This technique works great for bringing pelagic fish species within range. Richard Pillans A.K.A the mackerel whisperer recommends limiting the number of divers around the flasher as this can cause fish to spook (No more than 3 preferably 2).

Photo courtesy of Buzz Bomb Flasher Systems

26 // BETTER HUNTING TECHNIQUE.

According to Rob Allen flashers with small reflectors work better. In fact Rob says that during tests with large unrealistic flashers they noticed mackerel and wahoo turning away from the flasher early. Drifting with a flasher with a one up, one down method works great and you've got your buddy there for the second shot if you need it. Don't dive right on the flasher instead give the fish room.

Rob Allen also recommends swimming at the flasher and ignoring the fish if the fish comes in, takes a look and heads off. This action can make the fish think that there is something worth competing for and they will turn around for another look. Feigning a disinterest can also spark several species inquisitive nature. Turning away from them and not looking at them will often encourage them to come in closer.

Photo courtesy of Jessie Cripps

Photo courtesy of Jessie Cripps

27 // BETTER HUNTING TECHNIQUE.

Burley. Shrek and I have noticed that burley from oily fish works great at attracting pelagic fish onto the scene and we will often work a burley trail alongside our flashers.

An oily fish like mackerel can be cubed up with your dive knife and allowed to drift through the water column but be warned it can also attract sharks to the area. So experiment with different burley for different species. Invest in a burley bag and have it full before you jump in the water, use the fish frames (and viscera) from your last trip.

> "KEEP IT CONSTANT AND PROLONGED BUT NOT TOO THICK"
> — Chris Coates

28 // BETTER HUNTING TECHNIQUE.

Limit eye contact. Staring fish down will make them nervous. How nervous? Well in the words of Australian Rugby player Nick Cummins "As nervous as a gypsy with a mortgage". That's as bad as it gets and as fish can move at close to the speed of light, it's best to keep them calm so you can get a decent shot off. Mackerel, Yellowtail Kingfish, Samson Fish, and Wahoo will often circle you so if you can't get a shot away, stay calm as the fish might just come around again. Try keeping your head down and looking up through your mask to conceal your eyes. Predicting the path of the fish and extending the gun to where you think the fish will be is another tactic to reduce spooking the fish.

29 // BETTER HUNTING TECHNIQUE.

Posture and movement can create curiosity in fish. Pelagic fish can be attracted to a diver behaving unusually (so long as it's non-threatening). Diving at a flasher instead of at the fish is an example of this. Another good technique for many fish is feigning complete disinterest and even turning in the opposite direction and slowly moving off will arouse their curiosity.

30 // BETTER HUNTING TECHNIQUE.

Free Burley. Unless you are on an extended dive trip or in shark infested water, the guts from dispatched fish makes for great burley. Often other fish of the same species will become interested as what that fish has been eating will be in its digestive tract. In this way what you begin to burley will be exactly what they want to eat. This has worked well on large flighty Parrot fish and Spangled Emperor.

CHAPTER 4
Tips For Overcoming Common Difficulties

31 // COMMON DIFFICULTIES

Leg Cramping. Cramps can be a real problem for spearo's. Quite often cramps can happen towards the end of the day when we are fatigued or dehydrated. Cramps can grab you all of a sudden mid-water and cause significant pain. This is another reason to dive with a buddy because if you encounter seizing pain on the way up, an alert buddy will drop down and assist you back to the surface. It's not something that happens often but it's another buddy bonus.

Your dive buddy can also help you to stretch out the cramp by holding the corresponding heel in one hand and slowly pushing the end of the fin back towards your leg with the other hand. I know this helps with calf, foot and ankle cramp. Spearfishing.com.au in a related blog post suggests that keeping your electrolytes and hydration up during the day minimizes your chances for cramping. They also mention that potassium, calcium and magnesium supplementation can help prevent cramps however only consider supplementation under medical advice.

32 // COMMON DIFFICULTIES

Preventing and dealing with seasickness. Keep a really good eye on the weather forecast and get as much information on the conditions as you can, so you can decide whether you should go diving or not. I often turn down really rough days because I know I'm not going to enjoy myself. It is important to take your sea sick pills an hour before you hit the water. Sea sick pills don't work at all if you can't keep them down. Get your suit on and gear up before you get on the boat or out of the harbour. Nothing gets you sicker faster than being head down in your dive bag while the boat is rocking. Another tip to prevent seasickness is to stay at the stern of the boat, get low and central. Not only will your spine thank you but it's also the least rough part of the boat.

33 // COMMON DIFFICULTIES

Preventing and dealing with seasickness. Get in the water as quick as you can and leave the boat duties to those made of tougher stuff. The longer you spend on a rocking boat the more likely it is that you'll get sick. Focus on the horizon or land. This doesn't seem to work for me but it's something everyone suggests so I chucked it in (no pun intended). Stay positive and try not to focus on getting sick. Learn the early signs of getting sick. I start to burp and get gassy. This is the signal for me to go into damage control. Refrain from getting on the firewater the night before. Also sometimes the best advice is to just tough it out. The last two times I've been out I've been sick. So I just had a spew and kept on diving. I was the first to get in at every spot and I just kept going. I shot a few fish and lasted out the whole day. I plan on doing this more often in the hope of beating it.

34 // COMMON DIFFICULTIES

Pre Dive-Day Tips. 5P's = Prior Planning Prevents Poor Performance. The day before any trip follow a system to pack your gear, make sure it's in working order and it's all there. Check the conditions and make sure your vessel is in ship shape. If you sign up for the "Floater" email at noobspearo.com we give you a dive day equipment checklist. To further highlight the need for planning here is an excerpt from Ryan Belworthy A.K.A The Armed Snorkeler via www.noobspearo.com.

On one of my first shore dives I was away up in the Coromandel, New Zealand. I had only just gotten into the sport and I was really keen just to get in the water for a dive. On the morning after arriving I was up bright and early and walking down to the beach for a shore dive. Before I knew it I had shot a nice Kingie (Yellowtail Kingfish) and I was being towed round in about three meters of water with fairly heavy surge and rocks close by. I made a number of mistakes that day,

but the biggest one was assuming everything would be "sweet as". I failed to check the conditions so I got fairly pummelled swimming out through the surf. I also made the mistake of going by myself. I had never dived that area nor had I ever shot a Kingfish so admittedly I screwed up royally there. To top all that off, my gun was only 90cm and my float line was poor quality, too long and attached to a small buoy much like you see attached to crayfish pots. As you can gather it's probably somewhat of a miracle it didn't go extremely pear shaped. Nevertheless after nearly getting wrapped up, washed onto the rocks and dragged around, I found myself swimming back into shore having landed the Kingfish. I could talk about the potential hazards of all the mistakes I made that day, but the biggest thing I must emphasize is don't assume "she'll be right, spearfishing is not the sport for assuming all will be "sweet". **Be organized!**

a tip...
"THE DAY BEFORE
DIVING AVOID DAIRY
AND ALCOHOL. "

Equalising is a major problem for many spearo's. The day before diving avoid dairy and alcohol. Dairy encourages mucus production which can complicate equalizing and alcohol can cause severe dehydration. The common cold or flu (particularly the man cold) can cause mucus production and make equalising difficult. Many divers use pseudoephedrine to treat nasal, sinus and eustachian congestion. Consult a doctor to make sure this method is suitable for you.

Photo courtesy of Ben Rennie

CHAPTER 5
Advantages Of Joining a Spearfishing Community

Photo courtesy of Jessie Cripps

36 // SPEARFISHING COMMUNITY.

Shrek's experience: When I was just starting spearfishing, I went into the Adreno Spearfishing Store in Woolloongabba, Brisbane with an idea and wallet to match that I was going to get setup with equipment as cheaply as possible. Heading into their store a speargun was top of my list and so I made a bee-line straight to the speargun rack where a salesperson approached me and started to chat to me. He seemed to take a genuine interest in helping me get started spearfishing and so I listened attentively to his recommendations. He told me exactly what gun he thought I should buy and gave compelling reasons for why that was the gun he was recommending. However being cheap and wanting to save money, I bought a cheaper gun (the gun he recommended cost $100 more than the one I purchased), 9 months later I ended up buying the exact type of gun he had initially advised.

Be smart and do your homework, but listen to experienced retailer's advice. Tell them what you think your needs are and listen to what they have to say. It will save you in the long term and if they don't give you the advice you need go somewhere where they will look after you.

"...FIND YOURSELF A GOOD RETAILER AND SOMEONE THAT'S GOING TO SELL YOU A SPEARGUN AND A WETSUIT THAT ACTUALLY USES A SPEARGUN AND A WETSUIT. I THINK BUILD A GOOD RELATIONSHIP WITH THOSE PEOPLE. FACE TO FACE CONTACT IS FANTASTIC IF YOU CAN. I CAN'T RECOMMEND IT HIGHLY ENOUGH. A GOOD RETAILER SHOULD BE SELLING YOU GOOD GEAR. IF YOU BUY WISELY NOW, IT'S GOING TO SAVE YOU A LOT OF MONEY IN THE FUTURE. SO DON'T BUY A HUNDRED DOLLAR POP GUN WHEN IN SIX MONTHS' TIME, FROM WATCHING YOUTUBE TUTORIALS ON HOW TO SPEARFISH, OR COMING TO DO COURSES, YOU'LL WANT A 1.3 ROB ALLEN OR 1.1 ROB ALLEN, WHATEVER. SORRY FOR NAMING BRANDS, BUT THAT SEEMS TO BE THE GENERIC. BUT YEAH WHATEVER THE HORSES FOR COURSES ARE IN YOUR AREA. YOU REALIZE, SHIT I'VE JUST SPENT $500 ON A GUN THAT'S JUST TOO BIG FOR ME, A 1.4M WON'T WORK. OR JEEZ, THIS 90CM CRAY BASHER I BOUGHT (WON'T WORK), I WANT TO GO SHOOT SPANISH (MACKEREL) NOW AND I NEED A 1.4. SO GET GOOD GEAR AND TAKE THE RETAILER'S ADVICE."

— Simon Trippe

37 // SPEARFISHING COMMUNITY.

Experienced spearo's are a wealth of knowledge and will help you to improve. Most guys probably won't give you all of their secrets and tips straight away just because you showed up for a dive. Over time if you're persistent and do your apprenticeship, you will be rewarded with the tricks and tips that these guys have acquired over years. Facebook groups are another great way to meet like-minded people who are willing to meet up for dives and offer advice to new spearo's.

"FIND A COMMUNITY, MATE. SOMEWHERE THE EGO IS LEFT OUT AND YOU JUST GET THE ANSWERS, BECAUSE AT THE END OF THE DAY, WHEN YOU FIRST START OUT, YOU DON'T WANT TO SOUND LIKE YOU DON'T HAVE ANY IDEA. BUT WE'RE ALL IN THAT BOAT, SO YOU SHOULDN'T WORRY ABOUT THAT."

— Beau Armstrong

"JOIN A CLUB OR SPEARO COMMUNITY, FIND A GOOD MENTOR & LEARN THE ROPES. DON'T BE A DICKHEAD"

— Simon Trippe

Photo courtesy of Jessie Cripps

CHAPTER 6
Freediving Skills

Understanding what's going on in your body at depth is critical. From blood shift to methods for equalizing, it's all important and helps you to make better decisions. For example at 20m or 60ft your lungs are reduced to 1/3 their surface volume. Moving from Valsalva to Frenzal equalizing technique is essential for more comfortable diving at these depths. You will learn more about physiology and improved equalizing at a freediving course. Ted Harty at Immersion Freediving has helped many spearo's with equalisation problems through one on one equalisation training via skype.

Photo courtesy of Anvar Mufazalov

Do a freediving course with a reputable trainer who has a good understanding of spearfishing. Freediving and spearfishing are very different disciplines. Competitive freediving whether in the pool or the ocean is about singular events that are conducted in controlled environments. Recreational freediving is more about the experience, staying relaxed and enjoying each dive. Spearfishing is hunting underwater on repeated dives in uncontrolled environments using freediving techniques.

For these reasons we recommend doing a freediving course with an instructor who has a personal background with spearfishing. The benefits for doing a freediving course are multiple and there is no other single event that you could do to improve your spearfishing. Lately FII has developed a Freedive spearfishing course similar to a course Simon Trippe and Andrew Harvey conduct through Apnea Australia. These courses are something I wish were around when I started.

Photo courtesy of Immersion Freediving

IMMERSION
FREEDIVING

40 // FREEDIVING SKILLS.

One of the main things you learn in freediving courses is breathing. From avoiding hyperventilation to learning how to "three stage breathe" to surface recovery breathing, there is a lot to breathing and there is no doubt that this is an essential component to Freedive spearfishing.

Do you break your breathing into 3 stages? The first thing to expand when you breathe properly is your stomach, followed by your chest and finally the top of your lungs gently pulling the shoulders back to fill your throat and lungs. It's easy to write this down but the full realisation of this technique that you get on a freediving course will help you understand this to a much greater extent.

41 // FREEDIVING SKILLS.

Recovery breathing is a must for all spearo's. This technique can save your life as many divers will black out after reaching the surface (often 20-30 seconds after). It is important to "hook breathe" as it may save your life one day. Hook or recovery breathing is a specific method for rapidly re-oxygenating the blood and circulating it back to your crucial organs such as your brain. Good freediving instructors will teach you this technique so that in the event of heading back to the surface on the suspected edge of a blackout, you can execute a few 'hook' breaths to potentially avoid blackout.

GET CLOSER

HECSAQUATIC.COM

Drill shallow water blackout scenarios with your dive partners, it may save a life one day. Before spearfishing I had been in representative swimming teams, a surf lifeguard, scuba diving instructor and spent considerable time in and on the water, so I (quite logically) assumed that a blackout rescue would be a fairly straight forward exercise. After my first 2 poor attempts in a swimming pool, I realized that I was mistaken. Seriously just doing a couple of drills made all the difference to my technique and might make a difference if I am ever called on to save one of my mates. This is another reason to do a Freediving Course.

 43 // **FREEDIVING SKILLS.**

Some spearo's Inhale the air in their mask through their nose on the ascent. This gives you the benefit of that little bit of extra air to breathe on the way up.

44 //
FREEDIVING
SKILLS.

Trigger your mammalian dive reflex during the boat ride out. To do this dunk your face in the water or wet the face with some sea water. Some spearo's will also exhale their air and hold their breath face down in the water. It is also a good idea to pre-stretch your lungs by doing some full breaths and stretching out your big muscle groups is a good idea as well.

45 // FREEDIVING SKILLS.

The following is from freediving instructor and spearfisherman Wayne Judge

"I HAVE HEARD IT SAID THAT THE BEST TRAINING FOR SPEARFISHING IS SPEARFISHING. IF THAT IS THE CASE YOU WOULD NEED TO GO SPEARFISHING 3 TIMES A WEEK TO GET ANY REAL LASTING GAIN. IF THE BEST TRAINING FOR FOOTBALL WAS A GAME OF FOOTBALL, THERE WOULD BE NO MID-WEEK TRAINING SESSIONS, THERE WOULD BE MID-WEEK GAMES. WHETHER SPEARFISHING IS A HOBBY, A SPORT OR A LIFESTYLE THE SPEARO STANDS TO GAIN A LOT OF ABILITY IF HE OR SHE THOROUGHLY AND METICULOUSLY TRAINS WEAK POINTS INTO STRENGTHS. SERIOUS SWIMMERS DO THIS DAILY. WHETHER IN A GYM OR ON THE FIELD, TOP LEVEL FOOTBALLERS ALSO TRAIN DAILY. EVEN LOCAL TEAMS TRAIN ONCE OR TWICE A WEEK, THEN PLAY THE GAME ON THE WEEKEND. SPEARO'S NOT ONLY HAVE TO STUDY THEIR QUARRY AND

TERRAIN, THEY ALSO HAVE TO DEVELOP A BREATH-HOLD AND ECONOMICAL FINNING TECHNIQUE. IT IS THE BREATH-HOLD AND GOOD TECHNIQUE THAT WILL GIVE THEM DEPTH AND DOWNTIME.

'BUT EXACTLY HOW DOES ONE TRAIN FOR SPEARFISHING? NO ONE HAS WORKED IT OUT.' WELL, YOU WILL BE HAPPY TO KNOW THAT IT HAS BEEN WORKED OUT AND IT IS NOT ROCKET SCIENCE. THERE IS A WHOLE SPORT SET UP ON IMPROVING DEPTH AND DOWN TIME AND IT IS COMPETITIVE FREEDIVING. BUT I HEAR YOU SAY, FREEDIVING IS ALL ABOUT ONE OR TWO DIVES A DAY, NOT MANY DIVES REPEATED THROUGHOUT THE DAY. PERHAPS THAT IS TRUE FOR A FREEDIVING INSTRUCTOR WHO WAS NOT INTO SPEARFISHING. WHEN THE PHYSIOLOGICAL AND MENTAL BASICS OF BREATH HOLD DIVING ARE UNDERSTOOD, IT IS NOT HARD TO DEVELOP EXERCISES THAT DIRECTLY IMPROVE A SPEARO'S ABILITIES. THE HARD PART IS GETTING THE ATHLETE TO STICK AT THESE EXERCISES AND PUSH THROUGH THE VARIOUS BARRIERS WITH GOOD SENSE AND SAFETY. THIS IS NOT ABOUT TURNING UP A COUPLE OF NIGHTS A

WEEK AND DOING A FEW LAPS. IT IS ABOUT WORKING OUT AND COMPLETING TRAINING PROGRAMMES DESIGNED TO GET THE DIVER TO APPROACH HIS OR HER BEST, DESIGNED TO HANDLE HIS OR HER WEAKNESSES AND FURTHER STRENGTHEN HIS OR HER STRONG POINTS.

A SMART AND EXPERIENCED INSTRUCTOR WILL SPEED THINGS UP WITH GOOD DIRECTION, INTERESTING EXERCISES AND THE APPROPRIATE SAFE PRACTICES BUT IT IS THE DOGGED DETERMINATION OF THE DIVER, TO SPEND THE TIME WORKING HARD THAT WILL MAKE THE DIFFERENCE.

IT ALSO MUST BE FACTORED IN THAT TO MAKE GOOD GAINS ONE MUST TRAIN AT 80% OR MORE OF THEIR MAXIMUM. A SPEARO SHOULD NEVER BE WORKING AT THAT LEVEL IN THE OCEAN UNLESS HE OR SHE HAS ONE OR TWO TRAINED SAFETY DIVERS WATCHING HIM OR HER THROUGHOUT THE DIVES. HOWEVER IN THE CONTROLLED ENVIRONMENT OF A SWIMMING POOL AN ATHLETE CAN BE WATCHED THROUGH THEIR TRAINING AND HE OR SHE CAN AND SHOULD TRAIN UP AND INTO THE TOP 20% OF HIS OR HER ABILITIES.

HOW FORTUNATE IT IS, TO HAVE POOL TRAINING FACILITIES TO USE IN THE EVENINGS. WITH A BUDDY OR BETTER YET A TRAINING SQUAD, USE YOUR LOCAL SWIMMING POOL TO TRAIN. ENLIST THE SERVICES OF A FREEDIVING INSTRUCTOR TO HELP PLAN A PROGRAM AND COACH IMPROVEMENTS. ONGOING TRAINING IS EXCELLENT FOR HONING GOOD FREEDIVING TECHNIQUE."

— Wayne Judge

CHAPTER 7
Spearfishing Equipment Tips

"Don't over-complicate your gear" Dive watch, Speargun Reel, 30m (100ft) Float line, winged 1.8m Blue Water cannon, GoPro, yep you guessed it, it's all extra or over complicated equipment that you do not need starting out. Even if you have been spearfishing for years, Keep It Simple. If you are shore diving, carbon fibre fins and a 30m float line (rig line) will quite likely get broken, tangled or just be a pain in the arse.

To avoid this, carefully take inventory of everything you use and if it's not giving you a clear advantage or benefit then scrap it.

The 15m floatline setup is the best setup when starting out. This consists of a simple gun, speedspike, 15m floatline and a float with a flag. It's a safe, robust and highly effective setup that most spearo's will never change. The float keeps you visible on the surface and gives you somewhere to rest while the float line allows you to play the fish when it runs. The speedspike is pushed through the eye of the fish when it's killed and the fish slides up to the float line. out of the way.

48 // SPEARFISHING EQUIPMENT.

Try to never add more than one new piece of equipment each time you go diving. Acclimatising to new gear takes time and if you are dealing with challenging conditions at the same time, you can make yourself extremely uncomfortable. Also, if you try a new piece of equipment like a roller gun be prepared for a learning curve. Turbo and I both recently started using rollers and have experienced lots of the problems and are only now (after 3-4 dives each) starting to get everything dialled in. We are now loving rollers by the way and will struggle to go back to conventional guns.

Another example of this is; you have a new dive mask and its slightly leaking water or repeatedly fogging up, this is enough to make you uncomfortable. If you have also added a new dive watch or GoPro to this situation you have complicated your dive to an extent that leaves no room for anything else to happen (uncomfortable conditions like swell, dirty water, sharks etc.)

49 // SPEARFISHING EQUIPMENT.

Use a rubber weight belt, it will slide up your body less and have little effect on your breathing. Your weight belt should be well below your stomach, and not impede a full breath. Some spearos use a cord that ties onto the front of the belt and travels underneath (like a G-String) to really keep it secure. Be careful with this as it can affect your quick release buckle. When you are wearing a thicker wetsuit consider using other weight ballast such as freediving vests as your buoyancy distribution might be poor.

Photo courtesy of Red Blakely

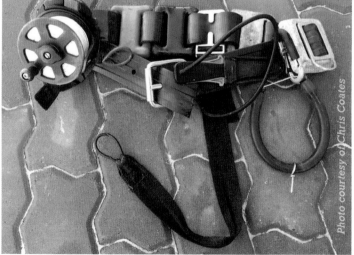

Photo courtesy of Chris Coates

50 // SPEARFISHING EQUIPMENT.

Bungees. A bungee is a length of rubber tube with a dyneema core that's used to reduce the shock as the fish takes up the slack when running and it can prevent tear offs. The bungee is usually connected between the float line and the float and can be vital in preventing a tear off.

Cameron's advice has some big implications as a bungee will stretch for up to 2 times its length and the tension gets progressively harder the more it stretches. This would gradually slow a fish with increasing tension rather than putting the brakes on too fast and risking a tear-off.

"OK SO WHEN YOU ARE HUNTING DOGTOOTH TUNA (IN DEEP WATER) ALWAYS RUN 30M OR 100 FT OF BUNGEE TO YOUR FLOATS"

Cameron Kirkconnell

51 // SPEARFISHING EQUIPMENT.

"JUST PICK ONE SPEARGUN AND STICK WITH IT FOR AS LONG AS YOU PHYSICALLY CAN, CHANGE LENGTHS BUT JUST FIND A GUN YOU ARE COMFORTABLE WITH. IT MAY BE SUPER COMPLICATED, IT MIGHT BE BASIC. I PREFER BASIC AND JUST STICK WITH IT AND YOU'LL FIND THAT AFTER A WHILE YOU WON'T EVEN HAVE TO AIM AT ALL, YOU'LL BE LOOKING AT THE FISH, AND WHERE YOU LOOK ON THE FISH IS WHERE YOU'LL SHOOT THE FISH".

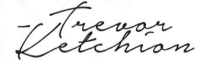

Chris Coates supported this advice by recommending that guys find a handle and muzzle setup they like and then just transfer it to different gun barrels. Whether it's upgrading to carbon fibre or changing to timber barrel, stick with the components that work for you.

52 // SPEARFISHING EQUIPMENT.

Reel Guns are growing in popularity due to the fact they negate a float line. However they run the risk of having the reel spooled by large fish which the diver needs to be conscious of. The final 15m (50ft) of spectra on the reel should be wound on very methodically (from one side to the other, one loop at a time). That way when you are playing a large fish and you get to that final 15m of line it will begin to spool off in a very orderly fashion alerting you to the fact. You can then either hook onto your belt reel or float line very quickly!

53 // SPEARFISHING EQUIPMENT.

Carrying two knives is essential for safe diving. Entanglements with old fishing line, float lines and reel line is a common and dangerous occurrence. Two knives ensure that at least one of these knives is accessible during entanglement.

Also many spearos will carry a large knife that is useful for chopping up fish for burley. As well as a smaller knife that is better suited to Ike Jime. Two knives are safer and have lots of practical advantages while only offering a slight hassle to carry.

"CARRY A KNIFE ON YOUR WEIGHT BELT SO YOU CAN GRAB IT WITH BOTH HANDS"

-Cameron Kirkconnell

54 // SPEARFISHING EQUIPMENT.

Keep your equipment simple and straight-forward, develop yourself and spend money and time getting out diving more. Also learn how to tie your own bridles and rubbers, crimp shooting line and patch your wetsuit as this will save you money in the long run.

"THE INDIAN AND NOT THE ARROW, THAT'S A REALLY BIG THING FOR ME. YOU SEE SO MANY BLOKES GOING OUT THERE AND THEY HAVE LIKE SIX DIFFERENT SPEARGUNS, IT'S ALL ABOUT THE GEAR YOU KNOW? TO ME, IT'S ALL ABOUT THE HUNTER. I KNOW BLOKES LIKE DWAYNE HERBERT, HE'S MULTIPLE TIME NEW ZEALAND SPEARFISHING CHAMPION AND I ASKED HIM WHAT HE USES AND HE DOESN'T EVEN KNOW. I ASKED HIM ABOUT RUBBER SIZE, AND HE WAS LIKE WHAT ARE YOU TALKING ABOUT? AND HE'S SHOOTING 40 KILO KINGIES WITH (I THINK) A 110 OUT OF THE 3 KINGS (ISLANDS). WHAT IT COMES DOWN TO I THINK, IS JUST GET A PIECE OF EQUIPMENT THAT YOU'VE BEEN TOLD IS GOING TO DO THE JOB. LIKE YOUR 120(CM) FOR NEW ZEALAND AND JUST GO AND HUNT, JUST GO AND TRY AND LEARN FISH AND TRY AND GET CLOSE. THAT'S THE THING BECAUSE THAT'S THE ONLY WAY YOU CAN BECOME A BETTER HUNTER. SO INDIAN AND NOT THE ARROW."

– Luke Potts

My Experience: I learned the hard way with cheap equipment and shore diving in dirty water, I have slowly improved my gear just as I have slowly been able to get better at diving and get out to better and better locations.

When aiming slow down and get the shot right. One of the hardest things to do when you see your first big Spanish Mackerel is to stay calm and wait for the fish to come into range so you can get a good holding shot on the fish. It's important to stay calm for a couple of reasons. Obviously if the fish is shot poorly it can tear off and will die. Secondly, a total miss will spook the fish. If the fish is out of range it's best not to take a long shot as there is a good chance the fish will return if it isn't spooked. This might sound like an easy tip but slowing down takes time to learn. Develop self-control, stay calm and slow down.

 56 // SPEARGUN USE.

When aiming at a fish using the natural shooting style (those that don't sight directly down the barrel) look at the exact spot on the fish where you want to shoot the fish, don't just aim for the middle! Be specific, even on large fish where you feel like you can't miss. When beginning however, it is better to use an orthodox method for aiming the speargun. With this method the diver sites down the speargun like you would with open sights on a rifle. When you become accurate replicate the aiming process. We will discuss where to aim in tip 58.

When shooting a speargun you need a firm grip and a stiff arm that is lined up with the target. The first rule of all marksmanship is to establish a firm position. Underwater this means a firm shooting hand as the recoil can pull your gun up and sideways skewing the shot. Like many of the contrasting behaviours we need to adopt in spearfishing, this can be another difficult one to learn.

A spearo must relax on the surface to bring their heart rate down, relax during the dive to conserve oxygen and relax on the bottom so as to not pose a threat to fish. After all that relaxation, the next step is to hold your arm and hand firm enough to provide a stable shooting platform.

For me personally as a 'feel' shooter my biggest misses come when the fish is so close that I think that I can't miss it and I fail to locate with my eyes exactly where I want to shoot the fish. I can't stress this enough - be very specific with the target your eyes paint on the fish.

Photo courtesy of Jessie Cripps

Shot placement. Many fish are incredibly soft fleshed and skinned. Couple that with their power and you've got a recipe for frustrating tear offs. This is why shot placement is so important. There are several places you want to shoot fish to avoid your spear from tearing out.

- **The first is the head.** With all that bone and tough structure the head and gill plate make for a nice holding shot that rarely pulls out. Not only that but if the shot doesn't stone (kill instantly) the fish it will slow it down considerably and the flesh won't be damaged in any way.

- **The next area is the spot between the dorsal and anal fin.** The flesh in this area has more sinews and is therefore much tougher which will give you a greater chance of the spear not pulling out. This is particularly true of the mackerel species.

- **The tail is also a common area for larger pelagic species,** in fact some spearo's swear by it as there is a lot of bone for good holding and they claim that it gives them great control over the fish's movement.

- **The lateral line on a fish indicates the location of the spine**, an angled shot close to this area will generally provide a holding shot and if you get it right you will hit the spine and incapacitate the fish instantly.

"GET TO KNOW YOUR GUN."
– Rob Allen

This follows an earlier tip from Chris Coates and Trevor Ketchion. It takes time to understand and use your speargun effectively. There are many facets to gun performance including tracking, range, maneuverability and recoil to name a few. Persist with your gun and avoid changing every time you miss. Develop an aiming system that works work for you and replicate it.

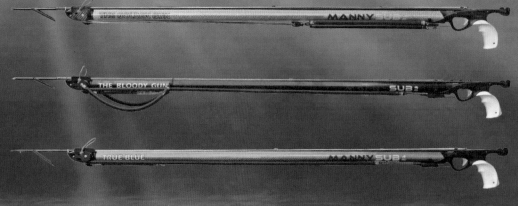

CHAPTER 8
Essential Skills

60 // ESSENTIAL SKILLS.

"Dive to your limits". This is a simple tip that we have heard from many experienced Spearo's but it's bloody spot on advice. Often if guys are diving right on the edge of their depth limits they will follow much stricter buddy protocols and only dive like this in clear, comfortable water and conditions. In my own crew when we are pushing our depth comforts we will dive in threes. Two up and one down. This way there are two guys immediately available in the event of a blackout and it also helps everyone to stick to the double surface time interval.

61 // ESSENTIAL SKILLS.

Focus and make small improvements to your diving. Develop your awareness in the moment and reflect on each dive as you breathe up. For example, you might be lifting your head as you descend in your eagerness to see what's around before you reach the bottom. To improve that, next time you rest on the surface watching your buddy complete their dive, pre-plan mentally what you want to do on the next dive. Think about descending without lifting your head. This takes discipline initially, but if you stick to it you will be more relaxed on the bottom and fish will be less flighty.

Anvar Mufazalov a freediving instructor in Cyprus has a great video series on YouTube called Deep Spearfishing Encyclopaedia; he talks all about focus and spearfishing hunting techniques in his videos. This learning habit takes time and self-discipline to develop but I can guarantee you will quickly become a much better Spearo and diver if you develop this mindset. If your buddy is aware of what you are focusing on they can also provide you with their opinion and advice.

First aid and advanced resuscitation. It goes without saying that spearfishing can be dangerous. Stings, bites, blackouts, boat strikes, the list goes on. It's important to know what to do to save your mates in case of an emergency. There are plenty of good first aid trainers around and some that are diving orientated. Get googling or check in with your local club for more information. The Australian Underwater Federation Queensland subsidized a First Aid and Radio Operators course for members so we went and got re-certified for $100. One of the biggest and probably most obvious takeaways was to **'Always keep a good well stocked first aid kit on hand'.**

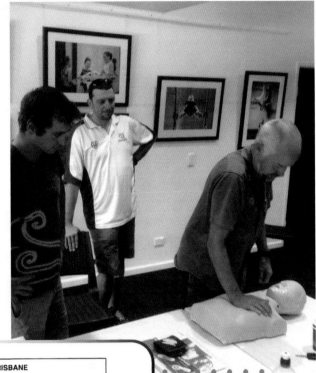

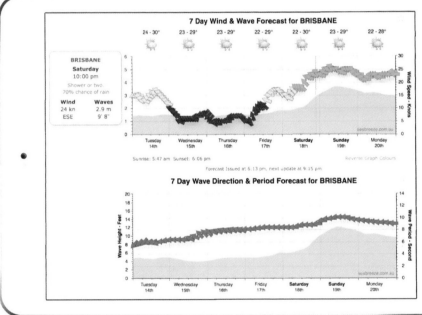

Keep an eye on the weather and conditions. A final check to make sure the weather is good should be done before leaving home. It's a waste of your fuel and time if the weather has changed significantly. Some of the locations I like to shore dive are 90 minutes drive and in the past I have arrived to brown muck and/or large swell but because I have driven 90 minutes I have often persevered in ridiculous conditions just because I had already made the ef-

fort. Being enthusiastic can often lead to diving in dangerous conditions. The sport is addictive but keep your wits about you when deciding whether or not to dive. Use 2 different forecasting services and monitor their accuracy over time. Two of our services use the same data but often come to different predictions about the weather. This way you can just go with the more conservative forecast (or at least split the difference of the two!).

Float line Awareness. Before and during your dive make sure you're not going to become entangled in your float line because this will cause tear-offs and frustration and or you can be dragged down by a large fish.

I have witnessed a mates float line get looped around his snorkel with a 20kg (45lb) plus Spanish Mackerel running for the hills and the resulting friction as it bound on the snorkel was a disappointing tear off.

Maintain awareness of your float line at all times, make it a focus and reduce the learning time. Float lines are still safer than reel guns for most forms of spearfishing starting out. If you are running a gun reel you should back it up by also including a belt reel to clip off to in the event of being spooled.

Fighting Fish. Softly does it. Naturally when something pulls hard you often instinctively want to pull hard in return. With many species that's a sure fire way to lose fish. Some pelagic species like mackerel and wahoo are clean fighters that prefer to run into open water rather than looking for holes and caves to dive into so there's no need to muscle them back to the boat. These fish are also soft fleshed and pulling hard can tear the spear out. Species like Dogtooth Tuna, Yellowtail Kingfish and Grouper are the opposite and if they make it to structure you risk losing your gear.

So with clean fighters and soft fleshed fish let them run and tire out so you don't risk pulling the spear out but for the dirtier quarry shot placement in a tough area is crucial so you can put the brakes on them when possible and steer them into favourable water. With Dogtooth Tuna this means big floats and short enough float lines that they don't bury you. With Yellowtail Kingfish a damaging shot and a good battle from the surface will generally do the trick.

Photo courtesy of Ben Rennie

Photo courtesy of Daniel Burns

Learn the local rules and regulations. Spearo's are increasingly coming under fire from poorly informed line fishermen and environmentalists for apparently doing the wrong thing. This is partly due to a small minority of idiots behaving poorly and giving spearo's a bad reputation. In this day and age it has never been more important to be seen to be environmentally responsible. Your local fisheries authority should be able to help with this. Here is a short list of rules to be mindful of in your local area, to ensure we can all keep enjoying the sport into the future.

- Size limits
- Bag limits
- No take species
- No go zones (green zones)
- Closed seasons
- Permits

67 // ESSENTIAL SKILLS.

Develop your fish identification skills. Unlike angling, spearfishing isn't suited to catch and release. Once you pull that trigger and put seven and a half millimetres of spring steel through a fish you can't really set it free to live out it's days. It's final and that's why your fish identification skills are so important. Knowing what species are in your local area and what they look like are the first steps in targeting your prey. Knowledge of fish species ensures you won't spear anything undesirable or worse, poisonous. It will also help you to gain a knowledge of the species you want to be targeting. Aaron Chasse in a recent Noob Spearo Podcast interview told us that to improve his fish ID skills he created his own book that catalogued all of the common species located in his area along with photos of each species taken underwater. He said this was a huge help in his early days.

Photo courtesy of Jessie Cripps

✓ | 68 // ESSENTIAL SKILLS.

Have and be a good dive buddy (be trustworthy). Love him or hate him you're going to need your dive buddy and they might just save your life one day. Your dive buddy is that guy or girl that you meet on the rocks on those cold winter mornings after they've already called five times making sure you're out of bed. They take photos of you holding up your catch and generally help to keep the stoke. More importantly they're on the surface watching you on every dive making sure you don't blackout and drown. A good buddy should also know the signs of blackout and be drilled in rescue techniques.

Photo courtesy of Peter Taing

 69 // ESSENTIAL SKILLS.

 70 // ESSENTIAL SKILLS.

Buddy Benefits. A good buddy can check your shot placement when you're playing a fish. Especially if you don't know exactly where your shot has landed. When you make it back to the surface after the shot, signal your buddy if you have any doubts about the shot and they can head down for a look.

If the fish requires a second shot, be patient with it. When sighting on the fish treat the shot as if it was in open water and not tethered. If the shot looks good however and it's not going to tear out DO NOT take a second shot as the ensuing tangle should be avoided if possible. If in doubt however take the shot. If it's your fish, don't be proud and risk the fish, call for a second shot.

Buddy Benefits Continued:

- Keeping watch for boat traffic while your buddy is underwater.

- Managing sharks together so that you land more fish.

- Having one buddy work the flasher while the other dives.

- The added security that you have in case of blackout, entanglement, other accidents.

- A mate to share the experiences with first hand and take photos with.

71 // CARING FOR YOUR CATCH.

Ike Jime is a method of humanely killing fish that originated in Japan. It is the method by which a spike is inserted into the brain of the fish usually behind and above the eye causing instant death. The fish's pectoral fins will flare and then relax which lets you know that you've hit the brain. Not only is Ike Jime humane but it greatly improves the eating quality of the fish as well. Instantly killing the fish stops reflex action like kicking and thrashing, which prevents the buildup of lactic acid that is said to sour the flavour of the fish. In addition, the blood in the flesh retracts into the gut cavity producing a better coloured fillet and improved taste. (to learn more visit www.ikejime.com)

 ## 72 // CARING FOR YOUR CATCH.

If you are on an extended dive trip (longer than one day), leave your fish un-gutted. According to former guest on the show Daniel Mann this can help to preserve the condition of the flesh.

Photo courtesy of Jessie Cripps

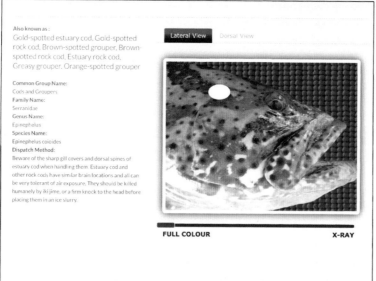

Also known as :
Gold-spotted estuary cod, Gold-spotted rock cod, Brown-spotted grouper, Brown-spotted rock cod, Estuary rock cod, Greasy grouper, Orange-spotted grouper

Common Group Name:
Cods and Groupers
Family Name:
Serranidae
Genus Name:
Epinephelus
Species Name:
Epinephelus coioides
Dispatch Method:
Beware of the sharp gill covers and dorsal spines of estuary cod when handling them. Estuary cod and other rock cods have similar brain locations and all can be very tolerant of air exposure. They should be killed humanely by iki jime, or a firm knock to the head before placing them in an ice slurry.

Lateral View Dorsal View

FULL COLOUR   X-RAY

73 // CARING FOR YOUR CATCH.

Putting your fish directly into an ice slurry will keep your catch colder and make for better eating quality. Make an ice slurry by combining sea water and ice at a ratio no less than two parts ice to one part water.

 ## 74 // CARING FOR YOUR CATCH.

When filleting fish sharp knives and lots of practice will eventually get you filleting well. YouTube tutorials can be very helpful when you are starting out. Get the whole crew into the processing of the catch to reduce the time it takes. One can fillet, one can skin and portion, another can label and bag. Labelling fish is a great idea as you can identify what fish you prefer to eat and when it was shot. Recently Turbo had a bad bout of Ciguatera poisoning and due to the multiple species shot, he had difficulty isolating exactly which species had caused the symptoms.

75 // ESSENTIAL SKILLS.

If you are just starting, try and head out for your first few dives in the best possible conditions. If you are a bit more advanced, be smart about when and where you try to make improvements and challenge yourself.

"... IF YOU'RE SOMEONE NEW JUST STARTING OUT, YOU (SHOULD) PROBABLY TRY AND JUST GO OUT WHEN THE OCEAN IS PERFECT, FLAT CALM SEAS, THE BEST VISIBILITY YOU CAN FIND, AND TRY NOT TO REALLY PUSH YOUR BOUNDARIES, YOU WANT TO TRY AND START OFF IN THE EASIEST CONDITIONS YOU CAN FIND"

— Doug Peterson,
AUTHOR OF 'SPEARFISHING, HOW TO GET STARTED'

Boat Trips. Keep It Simple - especially on your first boat trip.

When heading out on boat trips, your spearfishing gear should fit in one bag or plastic crate. Simplify it as much as possible, this will minimize the space you take up on the boat and you won't annoy the skipper!

. "...THE SIMPLER YOUR SETUP, THE MORE PEOPLE ARE GOING TO WANT TO TAKE YOU, BECAUSE IF YOU TURN UP ON SOMEONE'S BOAT AND YOU'VE GOT ALL THE BELLS AND WHISTLES AND A GIANT BAG, IT'S SPACE, IT'S NOT GOING TO GET USED, SO YOU JUST WANT TO HAVE A SIMPLE GUN, SIMPLE FINS. EVERYTHING NICE AND EASY, GEAR THAT DOESN'T BREAK DOWN ON YOU ALL THE TIME, AND YOU'LL GET A LOT MORE FISH AND A LOT MORE BOAT RIDES."

Trevor Ketchion

CHAPTER 9
Spearo 2.0

Pole Spear. Every now and then I go back and dust off the pole spear to re-hone my hunting skills. The limited capacity of pole spears means that the diver must develop better hunting skills to compensate for the limited power and range. In our interview with multiple world spearfishing record holder Cameron Kirkconnell he listed off several benefits including;

- Adopting better body language to get closer

- Reloading underwater after a miss

- Forced improvement with planning your approach

- Making the most of structure to give you the best opportunities

Enjoy the experience. I tell people that even if I shoot no fish when I go out (which sometimes happens) I never fail to have a good time with the lads. From relentless ponytail and kiwi jokes to blasting the music (Katy Perry or something similarly masculine) to dressing someone down for their last dive-day performance, the boys provide awesome banter as we head out to our destinations. I have been out on a few boats with people who don't even talk to you until you have 'proven' yourself in some way and it's never much fun. What a boring way to do anything, stay humble and as our mate Richard 'Snoek' Leonard says

"DON'T LOSE THAT FROTHING GROM NOOB STOKE, SO MANY GUYS ARE TOO SERIOUS. IT'S ONLY SPEARFISHING, REMEMBER WHY YOU ARE OUT THERE!"

Dive buddy. Look after your mates and be a good dive buddy. Often Spearfishing is such an individual experience. I sometimes get in the zone and forget about everything and everyone around me. I am so focused on myself, my immediate surroundings and internally relaxing that I forget about my dive buddy. When I realise, I look up and my dive buddy may be 75 meters away! It happens less now as I consciously make an effort but when I find myself in this position I either swim to my mate or yell out to him to come over to the good ground. I find that when I am being less self-focused I will shoot more fish for some reason, possibly because I am letting go of the single minded predatory body language. Either way my dive buddy is safer and we can share the good and bad times together

On a serious note, lots of people particularly young guys die participating in this sport. We become so single minded that we turn off our own internal safety checks so ensure you practice good dive buddy protocol. Imagine coming home without one of your mates, it's just not worth it.

Dive Log. Keep a log of every dive along with thorough notes. This might sound a bit tedious and boring however this will pay big dividends in the future. Seasonal variations of species, visibility and current are often regular and re-creatable scenarios. Here is a list of the type of information you might like to record,

- Date, time
- Tide, flood or ebb. High/Low
- Wind Speed and Direction
- Swell information
- Moon phase
- Water clarity or visibility
- Water temp (+Variance)
- Observations about species, benthos, rain in previous days etc.
- Keep an eye out for an official Noob Spearo Dive log in the future!

Photo courtesy of Jessie Cripps

81 // SPEARO 2.0.

GoPro. As many know the task of going through hours and hours of GoPro footage trying to find decent footage is a tedious business. This technique can save the editor time by allowing them to scroll quickly to the end of each clip rather than having to watch through every dive to see if there is anything worth using.

"WHEN YOU HAVE FINISHED YOUR DIVE AND ARE ABOUT TO TURN THE GOPRO OFF, INDICATE WITH YOUR FREE HAND WITH A QUICK THUMBS UP OR THUMBS DOWN OR THE OLD 'NOT SURE' SHAKY HAND TO INDICATE HOW GOOD THE FOOTAGE WAS, THIS WILL SAVE SO MUCH TIME IN THE EDITING PHASE."

-Michael Takach

Photo courtesy of Jessie Cripps

Time in the Water.

"HAVE A WHOLE LOT OF FUN, MAN. THE OCEAN IS SUCH A BEAUTIFUL PLACE, IT'S A MAGICAL PLACE, YOU KNOW. TRY TO KEEP THE AWE FACTOR, THE STOKE. NO MATTER HOW MANY TIMES YOU'VE BEEN TO THAT SAME CRACK IN THE REEF, NO MATTER HOW MANY TIMES YOU'VE DIVED ALONG THAT SAME GULLY. KEEP THAT STOKE, ENJOY THE OCEAN, IT'S THE MOST BEAUTIFUL THING THAT GOD'S CREATED AND HE'S GIVEN IT TO US. SO JUST ENJOY IT AND ALWAYS STAY STOKED ABOUT IT. AND THEN IF YOU WANT TO GET GOOD AT DIVING, THE BEST WAY TO DO IT, IS TIME IN THE WATER. THAT'S REALLY THE BEST WAY TO DO IT. JUST SPEND TIME IN THE WATER. LIKE ANYTHING WE DO IN LIFE, THE MORE CONSISTENTLY YOU DO IT, THE MORE YOU LEARN ABOUT DOING IT. AND YOU'LL FIND GUYS LIKE IN MY LATEST MOVIE, ONE FISH LEGENDS, (GUYS) LIKE BARRY PAXMAN, WHO ON ANY GIVEN YEAR CAN SPEND UP TO 250 – 300 DAYS IN THE WATER. THAT'S A LOT OF TIME. AND YOU SEE HIM TODAY, HE IS STILL SO PASSIONATE, EVEN ABOUT SHOOTING THAT 5KG SPANISH MACKEREL. HE'S SO STOKED."

- Richard Leonard

Photo courtesy of Darren Shields

"BECOME A GOOD HUNTER. YOU CAN BE THE BEST ATHLETE IN THE WORLD, BUT IF YOU DON'T KNOW HOW TO HUNT A FISH... SOME OF MY BEST MATES HAVE BEEN AMAZING ATHLETES, BUT THEY CAN'T HUNT A FISH. THEY DON'T KNOW HOW TO FIND THE FISH. LEARN TO HUNT AND THAT JUST MEANS SPENDING LOTS OF TIME IN THE WATER.

- Darren Shields

Dive with different people and in different places. If you only dive warm and clean water you will lack a broad skill-set and the adaptability that diving a variety of conditions provides. Every Spearo has something different, something unique that they do that gives them an edge. Dive with them and learn from them. Sometimes this means noting what not to do.

 84 // SPEARO 2.0.

Developing Awareness. Maintain a learning mindset and consciously develop your in-water awareness. By observation and analysing what is happening around you, you will be able to continually take advantage of opportunities that many fail to notice. Don't rely on others to give you all the information. Asking questions is great but lots of what you learn comes by observation and asking questions later.

For example it took me maybe 3-4 trips drift diving over reefs before I noticed that most of the bait and therefore the predatory pelagic species that I was targeting were hanging out over the front edges of the reef where the current hits first. So timing my dives so that I was in the right position (in the water column) as the current brought me over the reef was crucial for giving me the best chance at these fish. It seems simple now but in hindsight it's a really important observation that has allowed me to shoot more fish..

"... TRY AND UNDERSTAND THE SEA, THE SEA IS A UNIQUE SYSTEM AND WE ARE JUST THE ELEMENTS WHICH ARE IN THE SEA AND YOU CANNOT ENFORCE YOUR OWN RULES THERE. YOU HAVE TO TRY TO LEARN WITH THE SEA, THE CURRENTS, THE FISH BEHAVIOUR, THE TEMPERATURE, THE VISIBILITY, THE THERMOCLINE, THE WAVES, THE BOATS, EVERYTHING. YOU HAVE TO LEARN HOW IT ALL WORKS, AND YOU HAVE TO UNDERSTAND THE SYSTEM AND ADAPT YOUR DIVING TO IT"

— Anvar Mufazalov

 85 // SPEARO 2.0.

Peeing in your suit. There's no health risk to peeing in your wetsuit says spearfishing.com. au "Most people don't realize that urine is sterile, unless you have an infection of the urinary tract. The more water you drink, the less smelly your pee will be. The worst you have to fear is a case of diaper rash if the urine stays against your skin for several hours, and this too is less of a problem when your urine is diluted. Open your wetsuit under water and rinse it between dives." Therefore pee away I say, just make sure to wash your wetsuit thoroughly!

 86 // SPEARO 2.0.

Social Media. Modern-day spearo's are aware of the negative stigma that media has promoted and they are trying to change the public's perception by sharing the real spearfishing experience. Think about what you share from the perspective of people who are not familiar with with our sport. This will help ensure we can continue to enjoy our sport into the future.

a tip...

"THINK ABOUT WHAT YOU SHARE ON SOCIAL MEDIA FROM THE PERSPECTIVE OF PEOPLE WHO ARE NOT FAMILIAR WITH WITH OUR SPORT."

CHAPTER 10

Shore Diving

87 // SHORE DIVING.

"GEAR FOR SHORE DIVING NEEDS TO BE KEPT TO A MINIMUM. ENTERING AND EXITING DRESSED LIKE A CHRISTMAS TREE IS NOT ONLY DANGEROUS BUT YOU RUN THE RISK OF LOSING GEAR SHOULD THERE BE ANY WAVE ACTION. ALSO IF YOU HAVE A BIG SWIM EXCESS GEAR CAN TIRE YOU OUT FASTER THAN EXPECTED AND THIS COULD CUT YOUR DIVE SHORT. I HAVE SEEN DIVERS SO ENGROSSED IN SORTING OUT EXCESS GEAR WHILE DIVING THAT THEY ACTUALLY MISS SEEING FISH. YOU ARE THERE TO EXPERIENCE THE UNDERWATER WORLD, NOT FIGHT WITH EQUIPMENT THAT IS NOT REALLY REQUIRED"

— Darren Shields

Photo courtesy of Red Blakely

88 // SHORE DIVING.

Your Chosen Entry Point needs to offer you a clean and expeditious route to where you want to dive. Looking at the swell from right in front of it and observing the wave sets for 5-15 minutes will give you a good idea of where and when it's going to be safest to jump in.

The place where I regularly shore dive often has a good swell rolling in, so I get in around at a sheltered corner and have a warm up swim before I start. Many locations will have somewhere similar such as a gutter where the run-out current minimizes the swell, or a semi sheltered point to enter. Entering the water is usually the safer part of the dive and if it's difficult to get in, it will probably be even harder getting out.

All of your equipment should be well organised, wrapped up if possible and fitted tightly before you enter the surf zone. Once you have cleared the surf zone then you can unravel and start spearfishing.

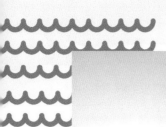

Photo courtesy of David Ochoa

 ## 89 // SHORE DIVING.

Exiting the water is the part of the dive that needs to be seriously planned. If your mate stabs himself with his dive knife and you need to get out of the water quickly, what is the plan? If you get bad cramp, will you be able to make it to your exit point? It sounds dramatic but these are the potential scenarios to think about when planning your exit points.

Entry points that were good for getting in the water, can be terrible for trying to get out due to many factors, prevailing current and swell behaviour among them. Therefore you should talk with your dive buddy while gearing up, and plan for a few different exit scenarios. If you are drift diving (diving with the current along a coastline) then you need to have extra contingency plans in case of emergency. Nothing beats local knowledge, the beauty of becoming a local is the awareness you develop of the area and contingency plans you have for when things don't go well.

 ## 90 // SHORE DIVING.

Move as quickly as you can when both entering and exiting the surf zone. Spend the time to observe the timing of wave sets, but when you have picked your time to go, Commit! and go for it, you have already made the decision and hesitation will just get you in trouble.

 ## 91 // SHORE DIVING.

Quietly and stealthily is the way of the Jedi Spearo. Good spearo's clear their snorkels quietly, duck dive quietly and move silently. Muffling noisy parts on your gear is a dive by dive conscious improvement and will make a difference to the volume of fish that you have an opportunity to shoot.

Shallow water spearfishing. In shallow water a spearo needs to be particularly quiet. In deeper water the distance between the surface and your prey muffles noise and movement and can offer the Spearo some advantage. When diving in shallow water this advantage is gone. Learning to hunt shallow is crucial and an underrated training ground for those that want to become competent underwater hunters.

This is something you will work on for years, when you head out spearfishing with experienced divers watch how they move and adopt the good behaviours you observe into your own diving.

Photo courtesy of Grant Laidlaw

Photo courtesy of Grant Laidlaw

a tip...

"ONE COMMON MISTAKE NOVICE SPEARO'S MAKE IS TO ASSUME THAT THEY HAVE TO DIVE DEEP TO SHOOT GOOD SPECIES – THIS IS UNTRUE, SOME OF THE BEST FISH ARE TAKEN IN LESS THAN 5M (15FT) OF WATER."

 93 // SHORE DIVING.

Different fish require different techniques however often on a surf beach the fish are close to the surf line. One common mistake novice spearo's make is to assume that they have to dive deep to shoot good species – this is untrue, some of the best fish are taken in less than 5m (15ft) of water. Again stealth is the key whilst maintaining an awareness of the risks inherent in diving in swell. When I started targeting crayfish (lobster) in Wellington, New Zealand I often made the mistake of thinking I had

to go out as far as I could to find them. In the end the best crayfish holes I found were only in 3m (10ft) of water (30+ crayfish in certain holes) and very close to shore. Large pelagic species are taken in shallow water also, Giant Trevally are frequently found in the shallows in Northern Queensland, Jewfish are often targeted in very shallow water here in Southern Queensland. White Sea Bass are regularly taken in relatively shallow water.

Photo courtesy of Jessie Cripps

 ## 94 // SHORE DIVING.

If you are in 6m (20ft) or more of water, head straight to the bottom and lay there as still as can be. This will sometimes attract fish. Their curiosity will force them to come and investigate.

Diving through a school of bait or undesirable species and laying on the bottom beneath them (without spooking the school) seems to make some target species much less cautious as you seem like less of a threat. Laying on the bottom is a more advanced technique particularly in deeper water. However as you begin to understand your body and its dive reflex this can be one of the most successful hunting strategies for both reef and pelagic species.

Laying there until you are blue in the face however is not a good idea, start with short bottom times and learn to listen to your body while staying conservative – be patient with your diving ability it takes time to adapt and learn.

Photo courtesy of Richard Leonard

≋ ⤳ // SHORE DIVING.

Marking the Spot. When you find that fishy spot or hidey hole whilst shore diving you can use landmarks and some alignment tricks to mark and remember that spot for next time. Line up on a landmark in the middle ground with something behind it in the background. For example; with your line of sight fixate on a tree on the shore line and line it up with an identifiable peak in the hills behind it. If you can manage this you will have a spot that you can find every time you go out. When the water is dirty and you have the slightest bit of current it can be hard to find that exact spot again.

If it is a hole you are marking you can also leave your speargun out the front and follow your floatline down to find it again (spearo's in Australia and NZ do this a lot when chasing crayfish or lobsters), this works in the short term, however landmarks are better for finding that spot next time.

CHAPTER 11
Bluewater Hunting Tips

Ditch the shark clip's and get D-Shackle's. Remove any and all weak points in your setup and KIS (keep it simple). In our interview with Cameron Kirkconnell he swore by 30m (100ft) of bungee before your float. Jaga Crossingham, Freedive Fiji Spearfishing guide however doesn't use this trick as he says they are often fighting blue water species in 30-40 metres of water and a Dogtooth Tuna will bury and destroy that setup as it gives the fish too much freedom to run for the reef. So use the bungee but only in truly open blue water conditions. Remove as many points of failure from your rig as is reasonable and practical.

Photo courtesy of Jessie Cripps

97 // BLUEWATER HUNTING.

Jaga Crossingham from Freedive Fiji explained to us that the main problem his clients have when hunting in bluewater is misjudging how far away the fish are in the open water. Jaga advises;

> "DON'T PULL THE TRIGGER UNTIL YOU CAN SEE THEIR EYE AND YOU START TO NOTICE ALL THE DETAIL, TAKING LONG SHOTS IS A WASTED OPPORTUNITY AS OFTEN DOGTOOTH IN PARTICULAR WILL HANG AROUND UNTIL THE FIRST SHOT HAS BEEN TAKEN".

It is important to resist the urge to shoot early when you first encounter a large pelagic fish. The fish will often come closer if it isn't spooked. New Zealand Spearfishing champion Dwayne Herbert calls the premature urge to shoot 'Big Buck Fever' which refers to deer hunting novices in North America on their first Stag hunts. It's something we can all get from time to time particularly when we see our first big pelagic fish. Shrek often shoots early followed by uncontrollable crying but he is currently seeking medical advice to help him out.

Photo courtesy of Jessie Cripps

98 // BLUEWATER HUNTING.

Bluewater hunting is a team event and everyone has a role to play in landing the fish. Roles include working the flasher, burlying or chumming, shark watch, second shot placement, boat driver and of course the hunter. Getting a plan together and sticking to it can greatly improve your chances of landing that fish of a lifetime.

a tip...

"KIS (KEEP IT SIMPLE)"

99 // BLUEWATER HUNTING.

Dispatching Large Fish. Always try to Ike Jime the fish in the water. Throwing a kicking 20kg Yellowtail Kingfish over the side of the boat with a shaft in it is not a good idea. You risk injuring your mate aboard, damaging the boat and at the very least getting blood and guts all over the place. Disregard this advice completely however when there is danger present from sharks.

100 // BLUEWATER HUNTING.

Boat Diving. Current. Good boaties are worth their weight in gold! When diving a reef in current a good boatie will position the divers far enough up current so that they can enter the water, get their guns loaded and be relaxed and prepared to drop on the front face of the reef early. This is often where most of the fish action will be and so knowledge of current direction and speed needs to be accounted for in order to allow spearo's the best chance. Once you have this track dialled in on the GPS plotter it's just a matter of lining up on the tracks from previous dives. Use current to your advantage. Some guys love swimming up current and it can put you on the good fish however you would be better off relaxing and going with the current so that you can have a longer more relaxed time on the bottom. Be like Turbo, use the boat, his pidgeon pegs can't handle the workload.

101 // BLUEWATER HUNTING.

Barracuda. Many spearo's have nasty scars and stories to match after shooting these fish. Although they offer a powerful fight and a good challenge to the Spearo, the eating quality is questionable and when shot these fish can cause damage with their razor sharp teeth. If they don't get you they could very well get your mate. Ask yourself 'if this fish worth the trouble?'

Aaron Bidwell	Bodhi oneil	Corey Hashimoto
Abraham Figueroa	Brad Gearhart	Craig Gush
Adam Frost	Brad Waugh	Cristian Andrei
Adam King	Brad witt	Dale Lewis
Adam Winfield	Brandon Miller	Dale Pearse
Adrien Simon	Brayden Francis	Dallas Robinson
Akeem King from Bequia	Brennan Lincoln	Dan Coursey
Alastair Gillespie	Brett Christensen	Dan Romo
Alastair Greer	Bri Van Scotter	Dan Walsh
Alex Hill	Brian Potgieter	Daniel Huie
Alex Miller	Bruce Lawson	Daniel Mann
Alistair	Bryan Russell	Danny Gallant
Alwyn Harrison	Cain Wiki Amelia Towns	Darien Rivera
Andrew Bortignon	Callum	Dave Watson
Andy Rowland	Cameron gall	David Ayling
Antonio	Carmel Greensill	David Gordo
Austin Barr	Carter Cox	David Hallamore
Bastien Finet	Chad	David Hayes
Ben Abram	Chee Ooi	David Mulheron
Ben Amrein	Chris Schlenner	David Smith
Ben Fleming	Christopher Smith	Davis Hanley
Benjamin Kurtz	Clay Groves	Denis Rizikov
Benjie Wales	Cody Halff	Don Kellett
BMW Girl	Cody Hallett	Doug Burdick

Dr Joe Keim

Duncan Henderson

Dustin

Dwayne Clechnch

Dylan Vanderhorst

Dylbo Baggins

Ellmo

Emmanuel Ontiveros

Evan Williams

Fran Plunkett

Frans Boeriis

Freya Greensill

Gabriel Pinto

Harlem Ratapu

Heikki Rauhala

Henk

Henrik Andersen

Henry Silvia

Hilary Ayrton

Hugo Pin

Jacob

Jacob Malakias Elmoey

Jacobus

Jake Lords

Jakk Hamilton

Jakob Glatz

James Codding

James Fisher

James Grant

James Murtagh

Jared Leonard

Jason

Jason B Adams

Jason Loui

Jason Panter

Jeff Garwood

Jeremy White

Joe Fernandez

John Rigsbee

Jon Weiss

Jonas Ostersen

Jonathan vail

Jorge Garcia

Josh

Josh and Anita

Josh chan

Josh Glenn

Josh Humbert

Josh Rosenblum

Joshua Porter

Jurg Kehl

Justin

Justin Poh

Justin Prazen

Kelly kemp

Kevin Daly

Kevin Guck

Kevin Smith

Kevin White

Kieran Denning

Kiernan McMahon

Kirsty lough

Kristian GS

Kurt Raymond

Lachlan Davison

Lael Aprieto

Lauren Sarasua

liam arstall

Lincoln Smith

Linka Jenner

Ludo Ln

Luis Romero

luke balkin

Luke Growney

Manuel Schwager

Marc Eskelund

Marshall

Mathew Hudson

Mathieu Peeters

Matt Fitz

Matt Mattison

Matt Newman

Matt Stewart

Matthew Cornish

Matthew Ramos

Maximilian Wolf

Mica Kentz

Michael Broner

Michael Hunt

Michael Huynh

Michael Wilborn

Miguel Ranzetta

Mikala

Mitchell Marriott

Moira

Moss Burmester

Nathan Beattie	Rob	Tasman Cranney
Nelson McKiggan	Robert Luiz	Ted Harty
Ng Ka Leong	Robert Porter	Thomas Jenner
Nic Launder	Rod Macnab	Thomas Mercer
Nick S	Ryan Allen	Thomas Sullivan
Nick Walton	Ryan arkelidis	Thomas Wakely
Noe Zartuche	Ryan E	Tim Doepel
NWsportsman	Ryan Fraser	Tim Greensill
Oleksiy Chaukin	Ryan Gattoni	Timothy Allison
Pat Mullins	Ryan McMillen	Toby
Pat Swanson	Sam Gaylard	Todd Kautz
Patrick	Sandro Pusceddu	Tony Brookbanks
Patrick Hallett	Scott Day	Tony Eynon
Paul Knepper	Sean Bear	Travis Corken
Pepijn Klijs	Sean Kranick	Troy
Prue Rennick	Shen Tian	Tyla Warrack
Quentin Peck	Skye Bailey	Tyler Betz
Rachid Zock	Spenser Ott	Tyrone Canning
Rangi Vallance	Stephan Whelan	Valentine Thomas
Rauno Lehtsalu	Stephen Hermon	Wayne Bulkley
Rhys Dixon	Steve Pogonowski	Wesley Cutajar
Ricardo Raposo	Steve Sawyer	Will Rawiri
Richard Kessling	Steven Keegel	Woody Fraser
Richard Ruberti	Stone French	Zane Turbessi
Rick Veal	Sven Franklin	

THANK YOU GUYS FOR HELPING US MAKE THIS PROJECT A REALITY

Shrek and Turbo

Summary

Becoming better at spearfishing is a lifelong journey, and at the end of the day every Spearo makes their own way in spearfishing. Our advice is to listen to other spearo's and experiment with their advice. You will develop much faster than someone who just goes diving.

There's no point in reinventing the wheel but not everything you hear is gospel truth so make your own mind up about things. Try to do it without having to learn everything the hard way. Go spearfishing as much as possible, but even when you are not in the water you can still be learning.

We hope some of these points will help you to improve your spearfishing. We won't give you a big safety spiel but we firmly advise you to use your brain and make good choices.

For more advice, wisdom and stories from spearos all over the world, tune into the Noob Spearo Podcast, you can find us at www.noob-spearo.com or download the interviews on iTunes or Stitcher radio. The Noob Spearo blog also offers stories, DIY articles, tutorials and further guides for the developing Spearo. Join us and share your experience!

Thank you to all the Legends!!

Thank you to all the legends that have been involved in the Noob Spearo. Without you we wouldn't be able to help the up and coming spearo's of the world. From podcast guests to bloggers you have all helped to make the Noob Spearo what it is today. You have shared your tips, tricks and wisdom with our audience and helped us all learn and improve.

For those that would like to be a part of Noob Spearo you can contribute by visiting **www.noobspearo.com/about/write-spearfishing-story-photo-contributor/**

This book would not be possible without the collaboration of the following spearo's. Thank you all for providing us with the excellent images found throughout the book. Weather you are a past guest or a spearo that offered us your pictures we thank you. You have all helped to bring this book to life.

Thanks to,

BEN RENNIE, GABRIEL WICKENS, JAMES YOUNG, DANIEL MANN, ROB ALLEN, BUZZ BOMB FLASHERS, RICHARD LEONARD, DAVID OCHOA, RED BLAKLEY, KEVIN SMITH

A special thanks to the following contributors, we couldn't have done it without you!

LUKE POTTS

Luke Potts is a New Zealand spearo film maker responsible for Aquatic rehab TV. Luke's no nonsense tutorials are a fantastic resource for all Spearo's. You can help support luke through Patreon.

https://www.patreon.com/aquatic_rehab_tv

https://www.youtube.com/user/aquaticTVrehab

TED HARTY

Ted Harty is a USA national freediving record holder and the founder of Immersion Freediving. Ted has been a full time freediving instructor since 2005 and has certified over 1000 students in this time. Ted is an industry leader and has coached the likes of Ben Greenfield of Ben Greenfield Fitness. Through Immersion Freediving Ted runs group and private freediving courses as well as frenzel equalisation sessions via skype.

https://immersionfreediving.com/

https://www.facebook.com/ImmersionFD/

JESSIE CRIPPS AND MICHAEL TAKACH

Jessie Cripps is a Riffe team diver, underwater videographer and photographer. Jessie currently holds two Women's Australian spearfishing records. Jessie is an avid writer and is featured in spearfishing magazines and blogs often with a drive to promote women in spearfishing. Jessie's photo's have been featured on the covers of Spearing magazine, International Spearfishing and Freediving, Hawaiian Skindiver and New Zealand Spearo.

Michael Takach is a commercial diver, FII freedive instructor and Riffe sponsored diver. Michael is a regular columnist in spearfishing magazines and he has featured on just about every spearfishing magazine in the world.

Together the pair are the founders of Underwater Ally their film production company that produces spectacular films showcasing their spearfishing adventures. If you would like to support the duo you can become a patron at **https://www.patreon.com/uap.**

www.underwaterallyproductions.com

DAVID OCHOA AND RICARDO NASCIMENTO

David Ochoa is an underwater videographer, photographer and film producer. David has worked extensively throughout the world for companies like Beachcam, Decathlon, Sheraton and Geotravel. Davis is most known in the spearfishing world for his work on the film Inhale, The Azores in One Breath. An outstanding film showcasing the Azores archipelago and it's spearfishing potential.

Ricardo Nascimento started as a water photographer with some of the largest surfing and body boarding magazines in the world. Ricardo has worked with clients like Red Bull USA, Siemens and Tourism Portugal to name a few. Ricardo now directs his own projects.

JEROMY GAMBLE

Jeromy is the publisher of Spearing Magazine, one of the world's most popular dedicated spearfishing magazines. To find out more about spearing magazine visit **www.spearingmagazine.com**. You can also listen to Jeromy via the noob spearo **podcastwww.noobspearo.com/noob-spearo-podcast/jeromy-gamble-spearing-mag**

THANK YOU FOR READING OUR BOOK!

3 QUICK REQUESTS

* For a free Dive Day Checklist, 10 More Tips To Become a Better Spearo, private Facebook access and more head over to **http://www.noobspearo.com/** and sign onto our email newsletter.

* Leave this book an honest review! It will help us reach more people like you.

* Join us on Facebook, Instagram, Twitter, Youtube and more.

You are also welcome to reach out and email us **turbo@noobspearo.com** or **shrek@noobspearo.com.**

99 TIPS

TO GET BETTER AT SPEARFISHING

ACTIONABLE INFORMATION
to improve your Spearfishing

BY ISAAC DALY AND LEVI BROWN
aka Noob Spearo's Shrek & Turbo